The

# of Reiki

A Beginner's Book for a Better

Understanding

By Lewis Haas

©2015

The Healing Energy of Reiki

A Beginner's Book for a Better Understanding

June 7, 2015

ISBN-13: 978-1508667278

ISBN-10: 1508667276

Additional writing contributions made by Gillian Billing, June 7, 2015

Disclaimer

Although the author and publisher have made every effort to ensure that the information in this book was correct at press time, the author and publisher do not assume and hereby disclaim any liability to any party for any loss, damage, or disruption caused by errors or omissions, whether such errors or omissions result from negligence, accident, or any other cause.

This is an informational guide and is not intended as a substitute for medical or professional services. Readers are urged to consult a variety of sources such as their medical doctor, dietitian or nutritionist. The information expressed herein is the opinion of the author and is not intended to reflect upon any particular person or company. The author shall have no responsibility or liability with respect to any loss or damage caused, or alleged, by the information or application contained in this guide. One Jacked Monkey, LLC, and the author are not associated nor represent any product or vendor mentioned in this book.

Table of Contents

Introduction

Welcome to the World of Reiki

This little book is designed to tell you about the fascinating Japanese healing form known as Reiki. Whether you're thinking of forging a new career as a practitioner or seeking a new way of getting help for what ails you as a patient - Reiki may be your solution.

Depression is a debilitating mental health issue that effects around 9% of the U.S. population[i]. I knew a woman who had symptoms of depression on and off since her teenage years. She had struggled with bullying, family issues and a low self esteem. As an adult, she was diagnosed with post natal depression, was medicated, then referred to a mental health specialist. After some time, her symptoms started to settle down. However the depression came back and after a few episodes causing more worrying symptoms like self harm, agoraphobia and suicide attempts, she was told that she would need medication for the rest of her life.

Enough to cause a dose of depression in itself, no one likes to think that they will be taking pills and going to counseling forever. She was unable to hold a job, her marriage was failing and she rarely left her house. Was this how the rest of her life was going to be? Well, this lady decided that there had to be more to life than that.

Through internet surfing she discovered the power of alternative therapies. She started meditating with a friend and learning about how the usage of color could influence her moods - yellow lifted her spirits, purple gave her confidence and red energized her body. She found a teacher who introduced her to other ways of healing and this led her to Reiki.

Within a year of investigating the art of Reiki, having treatments and starting to train in it, she had cut down on the pills, left the mental health counselors and was holding steady employment. She can testify first-hand to the power of Reiki and the lasting impact it has had on her life. Still learning Reiki, she now helps others with mental health issues from what she has greatly benefited in her own life.

Reiki is soft, non-intrusive, simple and peaceful. It may leave you relaxed, pain-free, emotionally released and mentally changed. It's a powerful art form and in this book we will explore the basics of it in bite-sized chunks.

I will explain:

1. The history of Reiki

2. The practice of Reiki

3. Reiki training for prospective healers

4. The effects of Reiki

I have tried to keep it in an easy, conversational style and you will finish this book understanding the basics of Reiki and be excited to find out more.

Reiki is a way of life, it can influence your relationships, your future, your food, and, as we have seen, your health. It helps you to be more positive and happy in life with five simple principles (see The 5 Key Principles of Reiki). You will be enabled to focus on what is important and empower you to help others.

Learning Reiki is truly one of the most beautiful paths you could choose to follow.

Reiki - The Universal Life Energy

Reiki means "universal life energy." When broken down, Reiki stands for:

1) Rei - God, Spirit, Creator (pronounced ray)

2) Ki - energy (pronounced key)

It is a practice steeped in history and has a lineage that goes back hundreds of years.

Reiki tells us that when we are healthy and well in the whole person (physically, mentally, emotionally and spiritually). We can feel stable, healthy and happy. If, however, something goes wrong in our personal world, this can make us ill in other ways, too. One issue often has a domino effect on the other areas of our personality and health.

This is better understood by looking at the mental anguish of losing your job. If you lose your job it may affect your mental health. You may lack energy and motivation, struggle to eat or sleep and your self esteem becomes low. Then you may show physical symptoms such as losing weight, catching a cold or getting headaches. Spiritually you may lose hope in the job market or faith in your own abilities. Emotionally you may become sad and frustrated. As you can see, you may think one problem affects only one area of your life, yet you end up with issues in all areas. This means you have become out of balance.

Energy is in all things. There are seven energy fields around us called auras and these reflect how we are feeling. These auras are linked to seven areas within the body that are known as our chakras and it is these areas that Reiki helps manage. As a spiritual art, it aims to heal these areas and balance them out (more on this in The 5 Main Elements and the 7 Chakras).

Reiki heals holistically, it touches each area and brings balance where it is needed. This, in turn, heals the fields that surround us, making us complete human beings once again. It is done by the laying on of hands from a qualified practitioner to the client. As the client, you will not have to do anything but receive the healing energy. It is a beautiful gift to both give and receive. Unlike a massage, there is minimum touch in a Reiki treatment. You stay fully clothed and can relax, warm and secure as your practitioner carries out their work in a gentle and quiet manner.

Reiki is not a religion and has no affiliation to any faith or central organization. It is a spiritual healing art dating back centuries, there is not a god, ritual or place of worship to attend. You do not need to join a club or pay a membership fee. Reiki is an alternative therapy that uses spirituality to bring healing to the body in a holistic way. It can be a way of life that enriches everyone by creating a well balanced and healthy environment.

The History of Reiki

The origins of Reiki can be traced back to 1899 when Reiki pioneer, Dr. Mikao Usui, went on a 21 day fast on Mount Kurama in Japan.

In Japan (1865), Mikao Usui was born to a wealthy family. Usui studied Buddhism and martial arts. He was a studious young man also well educated in philosophy, medicine and other religions. He later travelled to many countries in an effort to learn more information on these subjects.

When he grew up, Dr. Usui had several professions, and eventually became a Buddhist Monk. Dr. Usui was known for taking long periods of solitary meditation in an effort to further his research and education.

During the early 20th Century, Dr. Usui embarked on a 21 day fast on Mount

Kurama. It is said that during this time he had a spiritual awakening. And it was through hallucinations and visions that he was given the secrets to a healing art. This type of healing was akin to the laying on of hands that was believed that Jesus had done in biblical times. In addition, Dr. Usui's healing art would include words, symbols and mantras.

On his way down the mountain to civilization Dr. Usui stubbed his toe. He quickly took hold of it, as a natural reaction to the pain, and it healed immediately. He then went on to touch other people and they would be cured of diseases and illnesses of all manner - physical and otherwise.

Dr. Usui then streamlined the enlightenment he received and created the original form of Reiki. He developed the routine for the laying on of hands and merged a little of what he knew from other healing forms into it. He also established grading levels to help his trainees progress and track their learning from beginner to master. Dr. Usui was officially known as the Grand Master.[ii] There are now only 3 levels in Reiki - 1, 2 and Master (more on these later).

Dr. Usui found that his method of healing was inundating him with patients, so he decided to share his vision. It is rumored that although there were thousands of students over the ensuing years, only twenty of his pupils made it to the highest level of Master. Following his death the mantle of Grand Master was assumed by Dr. Chujiro Hayashi.

Prior to Dr. Usui's death in 1926, Dr. Hayashi was appointed to open a clinic and further his work. Hayashi had been a medic in the Navy and used this experience to also keep very detailed notes on clients, illnesses and their reactions to Reiki. He continued teaching and practicing in Japan until the outbreak of World War II. His reputation grew and he acquired patients from all over the world. He then passed the art of Reiki to a Japanese woman, Hawayo Takata, who resided in Hawaii.

Takata was treated by Dr. Hayashi for six months for abdominal issues. These included gall bladder, appendicitis and a life threatening tumor.[iii] It was believed that Reiki cured her ailments. She then stayed and trained in the healing art. Continuing the tradition, Takata taught approximately twenty-two masters and then passed it down to her grand-daughter. It was Takata who actually put the method down on paper. Although there may have been subtle changes to her records over the years, due to translations and misunderstandings, there is very little deviation from the original Usui method.

Over the years Reiki has been passed from generation to generation and has spread far and wide. If you choose to take part in learning Reiki, you will take your place in an ancient lineage of masters. It is considered an honor to be part of the rich lineage and it is a gift you will never regret being given.

The 5 Key Principles of Reiki

Reiki is a way of life and there are 5 key principles to live by. Dr. Usui was disappointed to find that people who came to him for help did not go on to live better lives, despite seeing this amazing revelation. He felt they should want to improve themselves and live more responsibly following a healing through Reiki. Therefore he created these 5 principles:

1) Just for today - do not worry
2) Just for today - do not anger
3) Just for today - honor your elders and teachers
4) Just for today - earn your living honestly
5) Just for today - be grateful for everything

These are valuable principles for life today. Just as relevant in the 21st Century as in any other:

1) Worry is a useless emotion that causes illness and physically manifests itself (such as ulcers). Although people naturally worry, try not to worry for just for one day. You may well find that you are more relaxed, at peace and content.

2) Anger is destructive and generally only damaging to the person experiencing it. It causes negative emotions and thoughts that spoil relationships and situations. Try for just one day to release all anger and just let it go. See how it feels to release your anger and live free of the aggression that goes with it.

3) Your elders, teachers, and parents are generally people who want the best

for you. These are people who want to see you safe, educated and well. They deserve your respect, so do not let the few spoil it for the many. Most people in authority are there to help and support you, so remember for one day to honor your elders and teachers. Be thankful for them.

4) We are all different with unique gifts to offer the world. Do things honestly and respect your boss, the work place and the rules. Taking home a company pen may seem very insignificant and no one would even know, but is it honest? Remember it is important to feel good about yourself, so be honest, respectful and true to who you are.

5) Be thankful, because there are so many things to be grateful for. I carry a note book with me in which I write things I am thankful for. My notes

start with family and friends, then job and hobbies. It has grown to include the weather, utilities, aid workers and inventors. It is nearly impossible being sad when you are being thankful. What a very powerful yet easy thing to be when you choose to be positive and happy through gratitude just for one day.

The woman I spoke about in the introduction found, at her lowest, it was impossible to think ahead any further than five minutes at a time. Part of her depression, she experienced no emotion when looking months ahead, even if it was to a holiday or special event. When she started feeling better, she coped a bit better and worked with one day at a time. She learned that things change very quickly, life is short and can be scary. If you do things for just one day, it's more manageable. You can give up smoking or drinking for just one day, be a little braver for just one day or maybe even go to a public place for just one day.

These 5 principles are more than just rules to live by, they are sensible recommendations for every day life.

Transferring Reiki Energy

When you hurt yourself, what is the first thing you do? You hold the area of pain and rub it better. When your child is hurt, what do you do? Of course, you hold your child before you even reach for the band aid. When a friend is upset, what do you do? Put an arm around your them and hold his/her hand.

Touch is what we do naturally when someone is in pain, that is what makes it so important. We carry our babies, we wipe tears and we give hugs. Touch is everywhere and it is often how we judge or understand people. My husband always judges men he meets by the power of their hand shake. I often find I am softer to people who give me a welcoming hug. Love is shown in affection, physical attention and making love. It's all about touch; there is healing in touch.

Reiki is all about touch. The energy is felt through the Reiki practitioner's palms and transferred through them to the client. The hands are where we have our sense of touch and whether we touch or hover they are still the transmitters of emotions. In religion, the hands are how blessings are given. For example, in Judaism where Moses ordained Joshua (Numbers 27:18/NIV), he used his hands. In New Testament Christianity, the hands are how the Holy Spirit is given to a disciple (Acts 6:6/NIV). Today, the hands are how spiritual healing is given - by putting a hand on the forehead of a believer.[iv]

Unfortunately, touch and feeling can be negative and painful. It can create fear and hate. Sometimes touch can be negative, such as a punishment or release of anger. In these instances the thought of touch can cause flinching and other negative feelings. Reiki may help with these deep seeded issues, but you may need some intensive treatments before you are able to think about becoming a practitioner. If you are the practitioner, maybe you will want to hover your hands above the body rather than actually make contact. This should be discussed thoroughly with a client before starting a Reiki treatment.

There is a routine to the laying on of hands in Reiki based around the chakras that is discussed in the next chapter. There will usually be some work done over the joints and any areas specified by the client. Time is spent on the feet to create grounding and security for the person as a whole. The feet link us to the earth, from where our energy comes. Grounding is simply a word that means you are linked with the earth under you. Often the practitioner will imagine roots from your toes going into the earth and pulling the color red out and up your legs to your base chakra. You may feel your feet heat up or tingle, possibly warmth in your legs. And, your mind may settle into a softer and easier stream of thoughts.

The Effects of Reiki

Reiki practitioner are not sacrificing anything physically in a treatment. The point of Reiki is for the practitioner to become a channel for the energy that flows through the ancestral line of Reiki Masters. The energy comes from the universe into practitioner, then they funnel the energy into the client. The Reiki practitioner delivers the energy through the recipient and to the appropriate areas of the body. It makes no difference if the client is open-minded or not. It is all about the practitioner being open to give what is being passed through her.

During the treatment, a practitioner may feel heat and tingling in her palms, heavy legs and often find time just melts away. It's therapeutic for the practitioner, mentally, spiritually and even physically. A Reiki practitioner usually feels their energy levels rise during the treatment and feel better after than they did before. It can be a two way street. The energy transferred into the recipient also helps the practitioner.

If you are the recipient, then you may feel sleepy afterwards, mainly from the relaxation of laying on a massage table. You could feel drained in an emotional way, yet energized and full of life. It can be like you turning over a new leaf and starting anew. The way you feel after a treatment depends completely on how open you are. Whether you are the client or the practitioner, you should both receive a change in feeling, mood and energy. Usually there will be some change in emotion following a session.

The 5 Main Elements and the 7 Chakras

The fundamentals of Reiki begin with the four main elements - Air, Water, Earth and Fire. There is a fifth element, believed by some to be an energy linking every living thing - from the tallest tree to the smallest insect, rocks, seas and animals. It is what joins us with nature and shows us the heartbeat in all of creation. We are born of energy and when we die, we go back into being energy and remain part of the living entity that is our universe. This energy is called Qi (pronounced key). It's the life force or spirituality that is at the core of everyone.

This universal energy is absorbed into the human body through chakras, shown in the form of auras surrounding the physical form. For a human being, there are seven of these auras and each field relates to a chakra area within the body.

They are channels that help distribute the universal qi to inner parts of the body.

Chakras are often seen as flowers that open up to receive the energy of the sun's rays to help the plant grow. Likewise the chakras open to receive the healing energy of the universe. This is a good way of visualizing the seven chakras. As you go through them, see a flower of the corresponding color in the area of the body it refers to.

Each of these chakras have a corresponding color both inside and out:

- The Base or Root Chakra is red in color, located around the pubic area, its aura is the closest to the body and holds to the physical shape. This chakra deals with the grounding or centering of a person. The foundation of a person, the Root Chakra is the start of being balanced in every way. Similar to the roots of a tree, the Root Chakra digs deep into the earth for security and nourishment while seeking nature's beginnings. Physically, this area relates to the kidneys, the lower back and the legs. Wearing red may help any ailments within these areas and establish a sense of unity to the earth.

- The Sacral Chakra is orange in color, based around the naval, and is the second field in the body. This chakra extends around the genitals and links to the sexual, reproductive and excretion organs. If you are trying to have a child for example, having reiki on this chakra may help and you could try surrounding yourself with the color orange.

- The Solar Plexus is yellow in color and is located just under the diaphragm or stomach area. This is commonly known as the "power center" and physically links to the spleen, the liver and the stomach. If you struggle dealing with strong emotions, having inappropriate reactions or hiding them away, this is the place for you to start. A lot of stress is held in the abdominal area and this chakra is often the most out of balance. Proper nutrition, hydration and self care are often suggestions for someone with solar plexus issues.

- The Heart Chakra is traditionally green and is in the chest. Sometimes seen as pink, the Heart Chakra is the place for self love, as well as, love for others. When all is well here it will improve your self esteem, relationships and level of empathy. In many ways, this is the most important chakra. You need to appreciate who you are, forgive who you were and accept who you will be. This all comes from the heart chakra and from here comes the passion and desire to help, support and heal others.

- The Throat Chakra is blue, located in the neck and is linked to communication. The throat chakra helps you, for example, speak clearly and get across what you want to say in a positive way. This chakra also enhances your creative self-expression, such as in art, music and public speaking.

- The Third Eye Chakra is indigo and between the eyebrows. The third eye is from where your spirituality and imagination stem. It governs the pituitary gland. As a writer or artist, this is a valuable chakra to focus on and can enable you to see things in a slightly out of focus way. If this chakra is imbalanced, you may suffer headaches, confusion and even nightmares.

- The Crown Chakra is indicated by the color violet and at the top of the head, the last and most outer of the auric fields. This chakra helps with the pineal gland. When balanced, this chakra helps with wisdom and knowledge. It is also known as the spiritual center where the blossom of the flower blooms and spiritual connection comes in.

In the Crown Chakra, you can pick up on atmosphere and energy that is welcoming and comfortable or doesn't feel quite right.[v]

Reiki is used to channel energy into these chakras through the auras where it can be used to heal whatever area needs it most. The practitioner may not know how or where any imbalance is but trusts that the universal energy is funneled through their hands to the right area. The imbalance or need can be physical, mental, emotional or spiritual. This is why Reiki is a holistic therapy as it deals with the whole body rather than just the area that is problematic.

The practice is often amazingly accurate and the feedback from a client often resonates so well with whatever the practitioner felt, saw or did. It is mind blowing.

Who Is Reiki For?

Reiki is for everyone. Whether you want to receive or train to be a practitioner, there is no boundary based on your sex, age, religion, color, job or financial status. It doesn't matter about your background or your faith, anyone can associate with Reiki and its simple message of healing. Reiki is an open-minded spiritual art using the energy of the universe.

There are several ways to find a Reiki practitioner for either receiving treatment or for learning more:

- Word of mouth

- Internet search for Reiki practitioners in your neighborhood

- Your family doctor may know of local clinics or centers for alternative therapy & medicine

- Try a new age, natural products, crystal shop - they will undoubtedly know someone you can talk to

If you want to learn how to administer Reiki treatments, you will need a Reiki Master. A teacher who knows their lineage, is passionate about their work and speaks with ease about it using their own anecdotes.

Should you be looking to receive Reiki as a healing for yourself, you will want someone who understands your needs, easily answers your questions and does not use too much jargon. They should be happy to sit and talk things through, explain what will happen and how to take things at your pace. They will instinctively know if you are ready for any Reiki training. Also when you are ready, the signs will be there to show you

- a strange thing to say, I know but, trust me, it's just the way it goes!

If you are thinking of learning how to give Reiki healing, you will need to know how long their courses are, how much they cost and if there are follow up support groups as well. Additionally, find out if you will get a certificate at the end of a course and if you can continue training to the more advanced levels.

One of the fundamentals of Reiki training is learning how to give treatment to yourself. Self healing is recommended and encouraged while you train. It will help you with ailments, relax you, aid in sleep and calm your stress levels. When you progress to more advanced training, you will learn how to send Reiki to people who are far away, even on the other side of the world, without laying hands on them. In Reiki Level 2 training, you learn how to reach people in the past and in the future with the aid of symbols. You could even use these symbols to put Reiki healing in an object to send to people that are ill. When they hold the object, they then receive the healing energy. There is no boundaries or limitations, so you can even heal animals.

Learning Reiki is a long process, so you must set aside time for developing your skills outside of the classroom. To grow as a Reiki practitioner, you need to research, study and spend time in personal space meditating and self healing. Reiki is done in 3 or 4 stages depending on the school you are learning from - Level 1, Level 2, and Master. Master is sometimes broken down into the advanced level (Level 3) and the teacher level (Master).[vi] This is something you may want to ask about at the start. The first two levels are usually completed over 2 days each and master levels take much longer.

Level 1 is an introduction for people wanting to learn more about Reiki and find out if it is something worth pursuing. Level 2 is for those who want to expand their knowledge and possibly become a practitioner. Master is the advanced level, requires extensive training and even more tutelage for training others. The Reiki Master will learn more of the background of Reiki in detail and introduce you to a deeper level of healing. It can be self-reflective and sometimes emotionally challenging.

There is at least three months between each level to adjust and to digest what you have learned. You may have to keep a diary of regular meditation and self healing practices. This can take the form of a 21-day cleanse following any of the courses. Some people find this time a useful place to start a new chapter of their lives - giving up smoking, exercising or eating healthier. However, it is mainly a time to practice self healing, meditation and keep notes of behavioral changes and dreams.

If you have experienced Reiki, but are not sure about the training, there is another option. A lot of teachers hold Reiki shares or circles, which are practice sessions for trainees of any level. They get together for a meditation, teaching and then a shorter session of healing where they take turns giving and receiving. If you know a teacher who hosts a Reiki share, then ask about an invitation. Often prospective students are allowed to come along to watch and to get treated. It would certainly be a chance to ask any questions and experience the atmosphere. This could be a valuable time to put your feet in the water and see if you want to go any further.

The Reiki Treatment

Okay, so you have decided to have a Reiki treatment. To start with, as the client, you may be asked to fill out a medical form. You should have a short talk about your life and what is going on with you, including your job, eating and drinking habits, your stress levels and any other relevant issues. This gives your practitioner a complete picture of you and how you may need support. The treatment process is then explained to you followed by answering any questions you may have.

When you are ready you lay on a massage table, under a blanket for warmth and a sense of security. You will likely be asked if you give permission for them to proceed and possibly even sign a disclaimer. You may be asked to take some deep breaths with the practitioner who will place their hands on your shoulders. This initiates a connection between you both. Then you just relax - go to your happy place, fall asleep, meditate, whatever eases you. Try to keep still and avoid talking. Yes, receiving a Reiki treatment really is that simple.

During the session you may feel some light touching but nothing should be uncomfortable or unwelcome. If your asked to turn over, just be careful and try to stay relaxed. You may feel some change in body temperature, a sensation of tingling or see lights - it is different for each client. It is all okay and working fine, as the practitioner channels positive energy through their hands into your body. They will be connecting to your chakras, filling and balancing them with energy and sending healing where it is needed.

It may cause you to remember or feel things that you have not thought of in a long time. In itself, this is healing and is why treating yourself with Reiki is often more important than treating others. Your practitioner will be sensitive to your change in vibration and will comfort, support or advise you as needed after the treatment.

At the end you will be asked to take your time in getting up and you can be helped up if needed. You should have time for discussing any feelings or thoughts you had during the treatment. The practitioner will give you feedback on the session. It's amazing how emotions are touched and memories relived through this process. Even little things such as a color seen in the mind's eye may be important. Don't hold anything back, no matter how silly you think it may sound.

A Reiki practitioner shared that on one treatment, she saw a woman in her mind while treating a client. She pictured this woman clearly: what she wore, the colors, accessories, how she was beautiful. Afterwards, she was nervous to mention this to her client since she thought it may mean nothing to her. However, she did share this information with her client. To her surprise, the client broke down in tears. It turned out that when she had instructed her client to go to her happy place at the beginning of the session, her client had imagined being with her deceased grandmother. Both the practitioner and client pictured the grandmother in her wedding outfit as she had worn to her marriage. They were both amazed and emotional - how wonderful to know that her beloved grandmother was with her in thought and in person. Especially as the client was in the middle of her own wedding preparations.[vii]

If there is a lot of feedback from the treatment, feel free to write notes or ask the practitioner to send an email with a summary of what was said. They would probably be happy to do this for you.

The Cost of a Reiki Treatment

As a recipient of a Reiki treatment, you will need to have a discussion about cost with your practitioner. They are people too and need to earn a living, however, most will scale it to your means. There should be an exchange of energies in some way and I have heard of cooking a meal, ironing clothes, walking the dog, administrative help or house cleaning as payment methods. All these actions are gifts you may be able to give in exchange for healing. A teacher sometimes will work out a deal, such as the first treatment free or book four treatments and get the fifth free. If you know you can benefit from Reiki and the practitioner does as well, you will come to some arrangement. Do not let finances put you off from getting Reiki treatment.

If you are looking to make a career out Reiki, it will not make you rich quick and the training is not cheap. Remember, it is a spiritual art form for giving a service of healing to others out of a sense of generosity and kind intention. You must go into it with a sense of peace and love for the people who will come to you.

Generally, Reiki treatment costs can range from $20 to $60 for a single one hour session. Prices vary from one practitioner to the next.

Reiki Healing for Enhancing Health Care

Reiki may not fully heal all that ails you. Please do not give up prescribed medication or any current treatments your family doctor has assigned to you. Reiki is a healing art but it is not a replacement for the advice of a doctor. That is not to say it won't heal you completely, however, it is more useful used in *combination* with medication. Scientists have come a very long way in creating pills and potions to help with symptoms, from headaches to vomiting. Prescribed medication and the advice from specialists, surgeons and general practitioners are invaluable and important for physical illnesses. However, Reiki deals with the holistic person - the whole from the inside out, that makes it priceless, too. Reiki is no substitution for medicine needed to regulate your heart rate or keep your organs working but it will deal with the emotional and mental effects of that illness. If you have a mental illness, Reiki is not a substitution for anti-depressants. But used in conjunction with your medications, it can help with the source of your illness which may be something buried deeply on an emotional level. This is where Reiki is invaluable and can cure on a deeper level than the pills.

No promises are made with Reiki. The practitioner is a channel for the universal energy to go where it is needed in the body. This may make you feel able to reduce your medications or change them, but don't stop taking them unless you have spoken with your doctor first.

Becoming a Reiki Practitioner

This is an overview of what a Reiki practitioner does in a treatment and does not substitute for actual training. Please see a qualified Reiki Master for proper training.

As a practitioner, you will need:

- To learn meditation

- To have empathy

- To keep an open mind

- And have a good understanding of Reiki

To be a Reiki Practitioner, you will have completed at least the first level of Reiki and will have confidence in what you are doing.

Before you give Reiki treatments, you will need to prepare physically, mentally and emotionally. Remember that Reiki is not just about you. Also spiritually, being in the zone is very important for this art, meditation will help you do this.

Prepare the space you will be using, assuming you are not working in your client's home, air the room and then clean, clear and cleanse the work space. Take out anything that is not needed, clean it and then cleanse using a candle, bell, water, incense or sage. This is not mandatory but rather a hint, to whatever your routine may include for making a room special and spiritual for you. Create a nice atmosphere that will induce relaxation and healing. If you are a Reiki Level 2 practitioner, place symbols on the walls, ceiling and floor.

Just before your client arrives, make the setting suitable for the treatment - use candles, some subtle incense, maybe some soft lights and music, too. The scents and sounds should be subtle, because no one wants to feel like they are drowning in lavender while listening to blaring music. Use anything that helps to induce relaxation and comfort for the client. Put away technology, turn off phones and keep animals out of the way if you are doing it at your home or the client's home.

Be sure people stay out of the room as it is important then to keep the space sacred for the work that will follow.

When the appointment begins, first fill out medical forms with the client (contact the doctor if needed) and have an informal chat to ascertain what they think they need from the treatment. Make this time cozy, relaxed and friendly, bear in mind they may be nervous and not sure what to expect. Do not rush.

During Reiki Level 1 training, you will be taught a routine for laying of hands. It is imperative that while you work, be aware to not keep an eye on the time too often that it distracts you. Similarly, when disruptive thoughts cross your mind, dismiss them and refocus on your client. As you work on an area, use your intuition and gut feelings to listen to your inner guide. Stay in a meditation state of mind and close your eyes, ask to be lead to where you are needed. Feel with your heart and mind rather than your hands. You may see things, hear things and feel things that are strange and unusual to you. They are nothing to be scared of. Relax, accept them and hold on to them for the end chat.

Depending on the routine you have been taught, when you get to the end of a Reiki treatment, you may be at the head of your client once more. From here, you stroke the aura fields into a balanced cover for the client and gently pinch the big toe to bring the recipient back to the room.

Do not rush your clients to move or to get up after a treatment. Have the final chat with them still laying down if necessary. Start by asking how they feel and how the session was for them. They may not say anything in particular as they may be too nervous to mention something that sounds silly or strange to them. Remind them that whatever is said is confidential and assure them that nothing is off limits. Maybe start with something you received from the treatment and go from there. Be sensitive to their emotions and do not be in a hurry to leave. They may have had a memory resurface or a long held secret that needs to be told. Be caring, sympathetic and neutral. Avoid showing judgment or surprise. Your job is to be a strong support.

It's a good personal touch to follow up with a note or email to confirm anything discussed with your clients, so they remember to follow any advice you may have given them. It's especially nice when emotions ran high and helpful thoughts may have not been absorbed. You have more time after a treatment to think and meditate on them more and put last minute thoughts on paper for your client.

As a last thought - do not practice Reiki if:

- You have been drinking in the last 24 hours

- You are on non-medicated drugs

- You are ill in any way

- You are not mentally in a good place, maybe you need a treatment rather than giving one?

Think of it this way - if you would not want to be treated by someone in the condition you are in - don't treat them. This is in respect, honor and kindness, to you, the client and the art of Reiki.

Reiki Attunements

When you take part in the Reiki Level 1 training, you will be given four attunements or initiations. The attunements enable you to be tuned in to the energy fields that you need to access to channel Reiki, which is a very specific therapeutic frequency.[viii] Initiation is an older word that is rarely used in the Reiki world now, but there are times that the attunements are referred to as initiations. The confusion that arises between these words are that, although initiation means beginning, you need to be attuned to an energy, rather than initiated into the Reiki practice.

To become attuned, the teacher will do a series of symbols and movements over you that will not hurt or affect you in any major way. They may move your hands and arms but nothing too dramatic. You will possibly feel "pins and needles" or a change in body temperature, but it will not cause you to lose your sense of where you are and what is going on around you.

This is not something to be feared, but something to be honored by. It links you to the past ancestry of the art form and helps your spirituality adjust to a new way of being.

The Significance of Symbols

In Reiki Level 2, you are taught symbols. These can unlock unlimited possibilities, not only for your Reiki practice but also for your everyday life. They pertain to power, emotion and distance/time.

During Reiki Level 1, you learn about energy, meditation, chakras and how to trust your own instincts in being empathic to your client. You learn the routine for giving Reiki to a client, how to give yourself Reiki and more about yourself and your abilities. You receive several attunements by way of an initiation that spiritually joins you to the Reiki world and opens you up to the lessons you are learning. These can be very powerful and cause changes within you, either in temperature or heart rate. Nothing can hurt you and if you never go any further in your journey with this art form, you are forever joined to this special ancestry. Reiki Level 1 is an introduction to who you are, shows you who you want to be and if this is a path you want to travel.

After Reiki Level 1, you can use the routine you have learned to treat friends and family. Complete Reiki Level 2 and you can take things a step further. You have the ability to work on animals, medicine, food and seeds. Additionally, you can send healing to distant friends, natural disasters, past and future events. That is the difference the symbols will make since they take the personal work you have done in yourself and help you send it out in time and space to things known and even unknown.

You can send blessings to your grand children, healing to your past self, forgiveness to the school bully, support to aid workers. You could also enhance the nutritional value in food, the healing in your medicine, place good wishes on a card and even put a symbol on your bed for a good night's sleep. Again, experiment with the many possibilities.

And, this is just a taste of what could be in the future if you choose to go a bit further on this path to Reiki Level 2 and Reiki Master.

The Importance of a Guide in Reiki Treatments

If you have never meditated before, this information may sound a bit out there. Your first meditations are normally guided by another person. They will take you into a deep state of relaxation and then paint a picture for you about where you are situated. You simply relax and focus on an imagined place. Guided meditation is a fantastic process to do and I advise anyone to experience it at least once. It is a very therapeutic practice.

Once you have done a few assisted meditations, you should be able to take yourself to that relaxed state of mind and silently guide yourself. You may choose to picture a guide of your choice to show you around, talk to you and give you gifts. Don't forget, it maybe your imagination, but in such a peaceful place it will be your inner self that is your guide. That is why it's important to listen to them, because it's your own deep down beliefs and they are usually better than the normal thoughts you have. These thoughts are not so polluted.

After consistently practicing self-guided meditation, you will get a better handle on how to access your own inner guides. Your inner guide assists you in the direction of your Reiki treatments. It should be simple for you to find your Reiki guide for when you come to practice the art. That Reiki guide works through you when you invite them in at the start of a session. You simply be their channel to bring healing, well-being and comfort.

The Power of Intention

When using Reiki, the most important thing is to put the client first. You are just the servant and the vessel of the universal energies. The power of intention is having the desire to be of service through healing and helping your client.

The recipient needs to feel cared about, focused on, special and important. Your intention is to help them and nothing else for the time they are with you. That is the power of intention - to make someone's well-being the intention of your work.

With that intention in mind, you can be a powerful healer. Before you even meet your client you could think and wish good things for them. You could meditate on them, ask your guides to help you with what may need your attention and make a note of any messages or thoughts that come through.

While you are using Reiki, the power of intention is to heal that person or to pass the energies of the universe to whatever part of the client's body needs it most. You are intending it to do good. If you forget the routine or leave out a hand placement, it's okay. As long as you are working with the intention of channeling the positive healing energy, you are still doing good for your client. This makes the intention almost more important than the healing itself. Don't allow a routine you have been taught to stress you out. Do what you can with a positive, good feeling for that recipient.

You can get a feeling for someone at first sight. That is why it's important for the Reiki practitioner to meet, talk and get a feeling for their client before the treatment. Once the practitioner knows what the client wants and have made good preparations for the session, things can't really go wrong.

Client Confidentiality

Confidentiality is a must in the treatment of anyone on a professional basis. Both the practitioner and client must sign a form to confirm the arrangements and that no information will be discussed outside of an appointment. As a Reiki teacher you will be totally professional at all times and that includes the paperwork when you get home. Confidentiality and privacy cannot be stressed enough.

The Reiki practitioner will keep records. When you arrive you will be asked to fill out a medical questionnaire, including: any illnesses, operations, scar tissue, skin issues and prescribed medications you are taking. You should be asked about your age, any back problems, possibility of pre- or post-pregnancy conditions and other relevant health issues. They may ask about your home life like what your job is, who you live with and how you rate yourself on a stress level. This gives the practitioner an idea of any emotional, spiritual and mental problems that may need concentrating on. Of course, they will be led by their guides but this talk gives them a starting point and an insight into your life.

These forms will be kept in a secure place and if you should return, they will be brought out to see how things have changed since the last time. If you come for Reiki regularly you may find a difference in yourself, physically or mentally. After just one session there may be no noticeable change, so this is a treatment that needs consistent application. Your Reiki Practitioner will advise you how often you should get treatment.

Conclusion

I trust that this volume will have answered questions that you have, and allayed some fears of what Reiki is. It has a rich ancestral history and is held in high esteem by many people around the world. You should have some idea now about going for your first Reiki treatment or registering for a Reiki Level 1 course. If you are still unsure, investigate a Reiki Share meet up.

The woman we started with in the introduction found that with Reiki her quality of life improved. It gave her focus, aim and a goal that simultaneously served others and herself. The heat that flowed through her hands when treating people was a reassurance that she was capable of doing something good. The positive feedback from clients built her self esteem. This lady still finds there are black days and she struggles with stress like the rest of us. However, she copes much better now with the healing energy of Reiki. Her new found skills have developed into her holding down a job, running her own small business and developing her qualifications and experiences in many other holistic healing arts. The possibilities for her are endless and the same can apply to you.

Thank You

Thank you for downloading my book and I hope you enjoyed it and found many things insightful. I would really appreciate if you would take a minute to post a review at Amazon.com on this book. I check all my reviews and love to get feedback (this is the real reward for me - knowing that I'm helping others).

Furthermore, you can opt-in to my Book Notification Group to get all the latest information on free promotions, discounts and future book releases. Go to http://eepurl.com/bfE46z to get signed up.

If you have any friends or family that may enjoy this book, please spread the love and gift it to them. View my other work at Amazon Author Central.

About the Author

 Lewis Haas is a father of 3 girls and a freelance writer. He enjoys daily meditation, exercising and spending time with his family. Currently residing in Tampa, Florida, his favorite time of year is winter when he meditates in the great outdoors.

Special Thanks

Gillian Billing for all your guidance and insight. Without your contributions, this book would've been impossible. Carol Langkamp for your assistance in book promotion and administrative assistance. And, most of all, the inspiration for this publication, Kaye Cox. You are a truly remarkable women who is making such a large impact in this world as a Reiki Master/Teacher. Your efforts will echo for generations to come.

References

[i] Lliades, Chris (2013, January 23) Retrieved from everydayhealth.com/health-report/major-depression/depression-statistics

[ii] Sandwall, Goran (1999-2009) Retrieved from reiki.nu/history/usui/usui.html

[iii] Brown, Richard (1998-2015) Retrieved from astrology.richardbrown.com/rek_takt.shtml

[iv] Church of the Great God (2015) cgg.org/

[v] Ellis.Richard/2002/Reiki and the seven chakras your essential guide

[vi] Howell, Pippa (2014) Retrieved from reiki-course.co.uk/traininglevels.htm

[vii] clients permission sought and given

[viii] Miles, Pamela (2012, August 4) Retrieved from reikiinmedicine.org/reiki-basics/reiki-healing-attunement/

Made in the USA
Middletown, DE
01 September 2017